O Holy Night

CHRISTMAS WITH THE BOYS CHOIR OF HARLEM

Pictures by Faith Ringgold

HarperCollinsPublishers

Amistad

AND IT CAME TO PASS in those days, that there went out a decree from Caesar Augustus, that all the world should be taxed. (And this taxing was first made when Cyrenius was governor of Syria.) And all went to be taxed, every one into his own city. And Joseph also went up from Galilee, out of the city of Nazareth, into Judaea, unto the city of David, which is called Bethlehem; (because he was of the house and lineage of David:) To be taxed with Mary his espoused wife, being great with child. And so it was, that, while they were there, the days were accomplished that she should be delivered. And she brought forth her firstborn son, and wrapped him in swaddling clothes, and laid him in a manger; because there was no room for them in the inn. And there were in the same country shepherds abiding in the field, keeping watch over their flock by night. And, lo, the angel of the Lord came upon them, and the glory of the Lord shone round about them: and they were sore afraid. And the angel said unto them, Fear not: for, behold, I bring you good tidings of great joy, which shall be to all people. For unto you is born

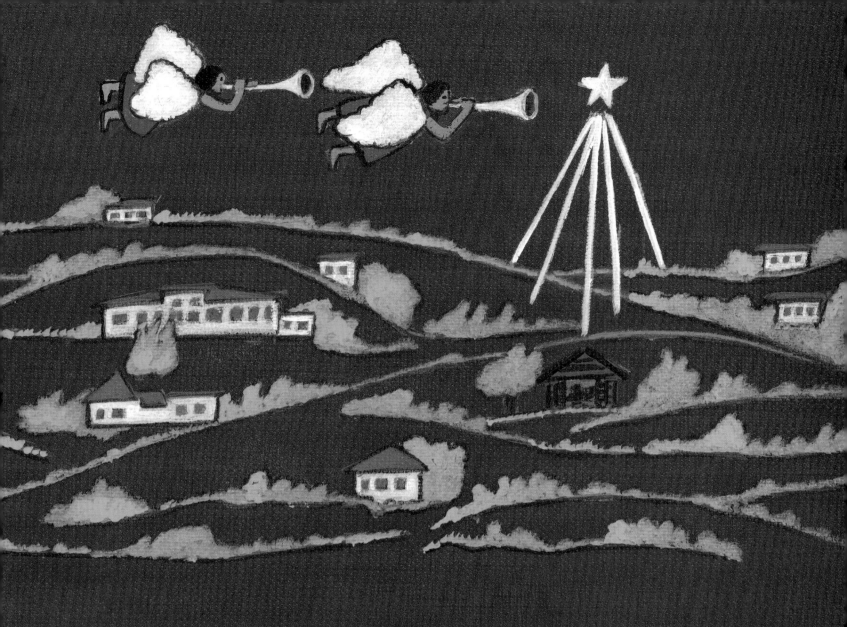

this day in the city of David a Saviour, which is Christ the Lord. And this shall be a sign unto you; Ye shall find the babe wrapped in swaddling clothes, lying in a manger. And suddenly there was with the angel a multitude of the heavenly host praising God, and saying, Glory to God in the highest, and on earth peace, good will toward men. And it came to pass, as the angels were gone away from them into heaven, the shepherds said one to another, Let us now go even unto Bethlehem, and see this thing which is come to pass, which the Lord hath made known unto us. And they came with haste, and found Mary, Joseph, and the babe lying in the manger. And when they had seen it, they made known abroad the saying which was told them concerning this child. And all they that heard it wondered at those things which were told them by the shepherds. But Mary kept all these things, and pondered them in her heart. And the shepherds returned, glorifying and praising God for all the things that they had heard and seen, as it was told unto them.

—Luke 2:1–20, King James Version

Silent Night

Silent night, holy night,

All is calm, all is bright.

Round yon Virgin Mother and Child,

Holy infant so tender and mild,

Sleep in heavenly peace;

Sleep in heavenly peace.

Silent night, holy night,

Shepherds quake at the sight.

Glories stream from heaven afar,

Heav'nly hosts sing Alleluia;

Christ the Savior is born;

Christ the Savior is born.

O Come, All Ye Faithful

O come, all ye faithful, joyful and triumphant,

O come ye, O come ye to Bethlehem.

Come and behold Him, born the King of angels!

O come, let us adore Him,

O come, let us adore Him,

O come, let us adore Him,

Christ, the Lord.

See how the shepherds summoned to His cradle,

Leaving their flocks, draw nigh with lowly fear;

We too will thither bend our joyful footsteps;

O come, let us adore Him,

O come, let us adore Him,

O come, let us adore Him,

Christ, the Lord.

Lo, star led Chieftains, Magi, Christ adoring,

Offer Him incense, gold and myrrh;

We to the Christ Child bring our hearts' oblations:

O come, let us adore Him,

O come, let us adore Him,

O come, let us adore Him,

Christ, the Lord.

Child, for us sinners poor and in a manger,
Fain we embrace Thee with awe and love:
Who would not love Thee, loving us so dearly?

O come, let us adore Him,
O come, let us adore Him,
O come, let us adore Him,
Christ, the Lord.

Sing, choirs of angels, sing in exultation;

Sing all ye citizens of heav'n above:

Glory to God in the Highest.

O come, let us adore Him,

O come, let us adore Him,

O come, let us adore Him,

Christ, the Lord.

Yea, Lord, we greet Thee, born this happy morning;

Jesus, to Thee be glory giv'n;

Word of the Father, now in flesh appearing.

O come, let us adore Him,

O come, let us adore Him,

O come, let us adore Him,

Christ, the Lord.

O Holy Night

O holy night, the stars are brightly shining;
It is the night of our dear Savior's birth.

Long lay the world in sin and error pining,

Till He appeared and the soul felt its worth.

A thrill of hope, the weary soul rejoices,

For yonder breaks a new and glorious morn.

Fall on your knees,

Oh, hear the angel voices!

O night divine, O night when Christ was born!

O night, O holy night, O night divine!

Truly He taught us to love one another;

His law is love and His gospel is peace.

Chains shall He break, for the slave is our brother,

And in His name all oppression shall cease.

Sweet hymns of joy in grateful chorus raise we,

Let all within us praise His holy name.

Christ is the Lord,

I will ever remember to sing His praise,

His pow'r and glory forever I will proclaim,

His pow'r and glory forever I will proclaim.

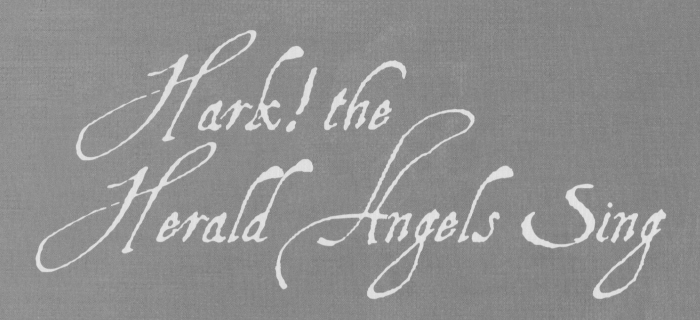

Hark! the Herald Angels Sing

Hark! the herald angels sing,
"Glory to the newborn King!
Peace on earth and mercy mild,
God and sinners reconciled."

Joyful, all ye nations rise,

Join the triumph of the skies;

With angelic host proclaim,

"Christ is born in Bethlehem!"

Hark, the herald angels sing,

"Glory to the newborn King!"

Christ by highest heav'n adored;

Christ the everlasting Lord!

Late in time behold Him come,

Offspring of a Virgin's womb.

Veiled in flesh the Godhead see;

Hail the incarnate Deity.

Pleased as man with man to dwell,

Jesus our Emmanuel!

Hark, the herald angels sing,

"Glory to the newborn King!"

Hail the heav'n born Prince of Peace!

Hail the Son of Righteousness!

Light and Life to all He brings,

Ris'n with healing in His wings.

Mild He lays His glory by,

Born that man no more may die.

Born to raise the sons of earth;

Born to give them second birth.

Hark, the herald angels sing,

"Glory to the newborn King!"

Joy to the World

Joy to the world! The Lord has come:

Let earth receive her King.

Let ev'ry heart prepare Him room,

And heav'n and nature sing,

And heav'n and nature sing,

And heav'n, and heav'n and nature sing.

Joy to the world! The Savior reigns:

Let men their songs employ,

While fields and floods, rocks, hills and plains

Repeat the sounding joy,

Repeat the sounding joy,

Repeat, repeat the sounding joy.

No more let sins and sorrows grow,

Nor thorns infest the ground;

He comes to make His blessings flow

Far as the curse is found,

Far as the curse is found,

Far as, far as the curse is found.

He rules the world with truth and grace,

And makes the nations prove

The glories of His righteousness

And wonders of His love,

And wonders of His love,

And wonders, wonders of His love.

Amistad is an imprint of HarperCollins Publishers Inc.

O Holy Night

The Boys Choir of Harlem chose five songs beloved for their spiritual vitality and timeless appeal. • Illustrations copyright © 2004 by Faith Ringgold
Manufactured in China by South China Printing Company Ltd. • All rights reserved.• www.harperchildrens.com • Library of Congress Cataloging-in-Publication Data
O holy night : Christmas with the Boys Choir of Harlem / pictures by Faith Ringgold.—1st ed. • p.   cm. • Summary: Presents the Christmas story according to Luke plus the words to five
popular Christmas carols—"Silent Night," "O Come, All Ye Faithful," "O Holy Night," "Hark! the Herald Angels Sing," and "Joy to the World," sung on the accompanying CD by the Boys
Choir of Harlem. • ISBN 0-06-000979-9 — ISBN 0-06-051819-7 (lib. bdg.)
1. Carols, English—Texts—Juvenile literature. 2. Christmas music—Texts—Juvenile literature. [1. Carols, English. 2. Christmas music.] I. Ringgold, Faith, ill. II. Boys' Choir of Harlem.
ML54.6.02 2004   782.28'1723—dc21   2003001820   CIP AC • Design by Stephanie Bart-Horvath • 1 2 3 4 5 6 7 8 9 10 • ❖ • First Edition

Wishing You Heavenly Peace

—Faith Ringgold and the Boys Choir of Harlem